I JUDGE YOU WHEN YOU

USE POOR GRAMMAR

A Collection of **Egregious** Errors,

Disconcerting Bloopers, and Other **Linguistic** Slip-Ups

I JUDGE YOU WHEN YOU USE POOR GRAMMAR

Sharon Eliza Nichols

 St. Martin's Griffin ❧ New York

www.stmartins.com

Nichols, Sharon Eliza.
    I judge you when you use poor grammar : a collection of egregious errors, disconcerting bloopers, and other linguistic slip-ups / Sharon Eliza Nichols.
        p. cm.
    ISBN 978-0-312-53301-4
    1. English language—Errors in usage. 2. English language—Usage. I. Title.
PE1460.N47 2009
428.2—dc22

2008042618

First Edition: October 2009

10 9 8 7 6

For my parents, who love me even when I don't deserve it,

and for my brother and sister,

who are capable of far more than they know.

CONTENTS

PREFACE

As evidenced by the three hundred thousand plus members of the Facebook group by the same name, I'm not alone in my contempt of the misuse of the English language. I judge people when they use poor grammar, you judge people when they use poor grammar, and we've probably all been the unknowing recipient of some other grammarian's judgment of our (extraordinarily rare, of course) poor uses of grammar.

Words are the foundation of our interaction with each other. They communicate definite impressions to other people, and this is especially true for writing aimed at large audiences, such as the advertising of big companies or traffic signs on four-lane highways. You've probably seen signs like those in the following pages and thought to yourself, "Somebody should have known better!"

Spelling and grammatical errors are far too common, but fortunately, the members of the Facebook group have a sense of humor. These enthusiastic grammar groupies have taken and uploaded some seven thousand pictures of signs with errors that capture outrageous grammatical, spelling, and usage mistakes that appear in prominent places. This book is a collection of the funniest and most ridiculous of those pictures. I hope you enjoy the book as much as I enjoyed putting it together.

ACKNOWLEGMENTS

First and foremost, I'm grateful for the providence of God. Thank you to my grandparents, who have loved and encouraged me over the years. I'm also appreciative of the many coaches and teachers whose love and support shaped me into the person I am.

I'm thankful for Neil Salkind, my agent, and my editor, Daniela Rapp, both of whom graciously tolerated my procrastination and taught me how to create a book. (Neil and Daniela, my parents also thank you—from their hearts and their wallets.)

Thank you to the people at University of Alabama School of Law who had faith in me and helped throughout this process. Specifically, Aaron Latham and Professors Scott England, Alfred Brophy, and Paul Horwitz all contributed in different ways to making this book achievable.

Thank you to David Lat, who gave me my first shot at writing professionally. Finally, I'd like to extend my gratitude to Helen, Josh, Nick, Paco, Justin, Robert, Gloria, and Stephanie, and to all the members of the Facebook group who captured the images in this book. I hope the final result lives up to all of your expectations.

(P.S.: If I left anyone out, my bad. Send the hate mail to the Facebook grammar group!)

I JUDGE YOU WHEN YOU
USE POOR GRAMMAR

One

FOOD

AND

DRINK

It's the Southern take on the French Bistro.

But evidently alcohol was allowed while creating the sign.

Yum, bowels and camels early in the morning!

It plugs up the sink *and* wastes precious coffee grinds.

Apparently, this is a common mistake. The plural of *knife* is *knives*.

FISH
&
CHIP'S
£3·30

Is the fish Chip's
or are the chips Chip's?

TARA
TERESA JANESSA

EARLY DINNER
* special *
* FROM 4pm TO 6pm
① small Homos plate
② soup of the day
③ chicken shishlik
   OR ground beef Kabab
④ served with Rice OR Fries
   salad pita bread and Pickels
⑤ soft drink (soda)

We're here, we want the early dinner special,
get used to it. And don't leave off the pickels!

Their hot what?

I need my apostrophe eraser. And my Z flipper.

Tea isn't coffee, right?

SINCE THE 5TH FLOOR HAS

NO MAID SERVICE,

PLEASE DO NOT LEAVE YOUR
DISHES IN SINK

HAVE THE COMMOM CURTESY
TO WASH THEM AND PUT THEM
AWAY.

So close to what you meant,
but now I really want to see
the writer of this sign curtsey
while fixing it.

Pick a spelling, any spelling.

Opposite: I shouldn't have to contemplate
apostrophes while waiting for my arteries to harden.

Don't let bad punctuation happen to good neon.

I hope they all went to ooking school.

CHEESE !

Slice of Cheese adds $0.30
To your sandwich

Cheese do not come on your
sandwich Cheese is extra
$0.30 a slice

Except Philly Steak, Philly Chicken or Quesadilla

Cheese! It *does* not come included.

We take everything BUT reservations here!

Does this juice taste like metal to you?

Opposite: *They're back* sounds far more ominous than it's used here.

Katie's legal! Now, the difference between *your* and *you're*. . . .

No apostrophe. For the last time: Apostrophe for possession, just an *s* to make something plural.

Go ahead, cheesecake, make them happy!

Come on and git it!

Take the bad apostrophe away and make the poor man happy!

Hole Weet bread for sale. I prefer mine without holes and only very little weet, thanks.

Breakeast versus Breakwest?

Two
∧

SHOPPING
SIGNAGE

Well, it is much easier to spell than *bouquet*.

This is a error.

Dad's gets an apostrophe, but not *grads*. They couldn't even make consistent mistakes.

iPod's available here

ASK IN-STORE FOR DETAILS

Ipod's what are available here?

As a beauty store, shouldn't you know how to spell *aesthetics*? Especially if you want to name your store "Salon & Aesthetics."

Those pesky behinds—don't leave without them.

Life's too short to struggle with which *two* to use. Learn it.

Ouch. Spelling mistakes can have painful results, kids.

No, no, NO. We will not attend your yard sael, your yard sail, or even your yard sayle.

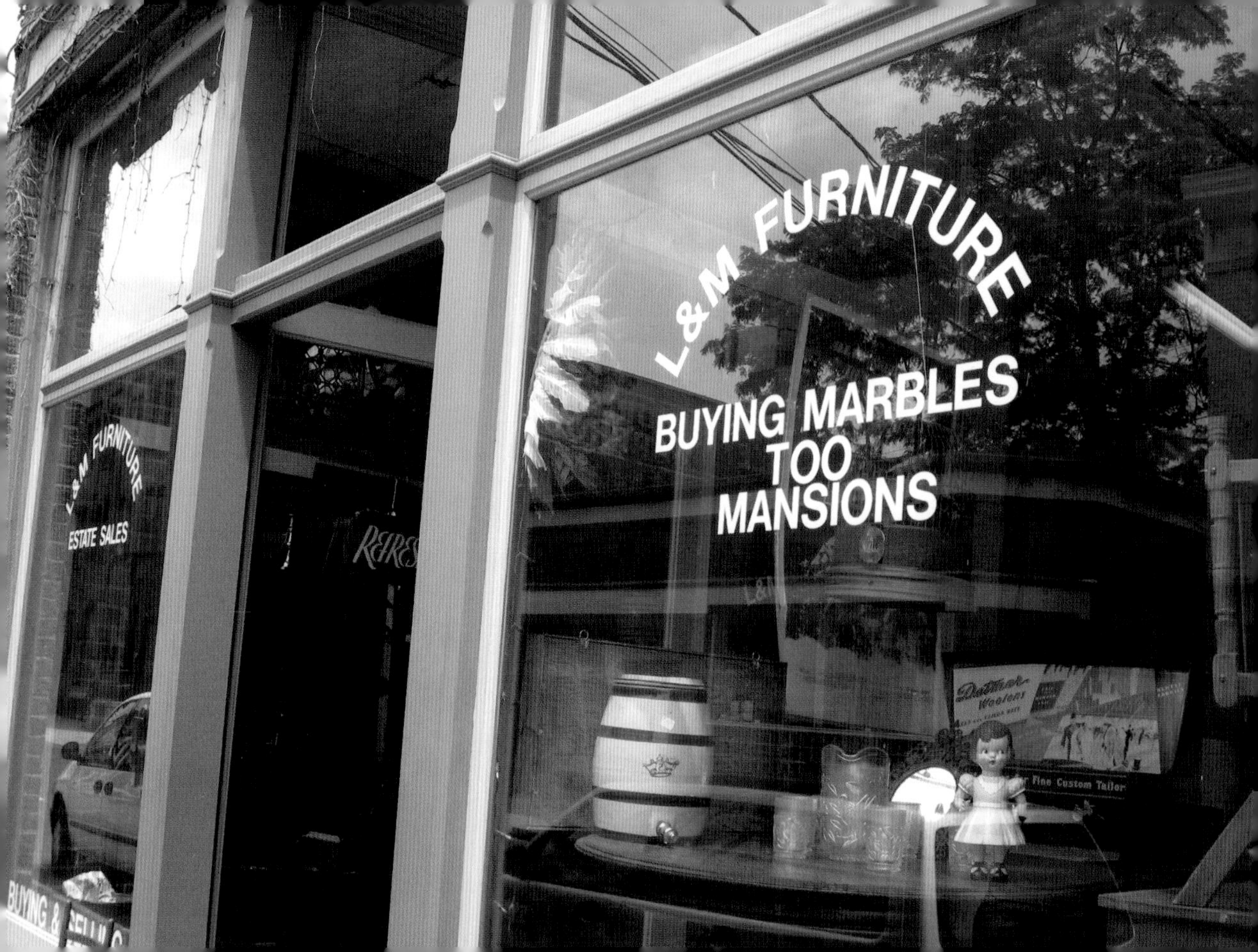

L & M FURNITURE

BUYING MARBLES
TOO
MANSIONS

L & M FURNITURE
ESTATE SALES

BUYING & SELLIN

You *are* local express store, and you *will* be open as normal. And you *will* use an apostrophe for possessives.

Opposite: Wanna buy an *o*?

At least it's not laminated.

There's more than one Brett?
The Cubby owns the toys?

APPLY FOR A FREE SAM'S CREDIT CARDS AND GET A FREE KEY LIME BUNDT CAKE TODAY THAT'S CORRECT THEY BOTH ARE FREE

No punctuation? Perhaps that's how
the store can give things away for free.
Expensive periods and commas!

Business,s
open as
usual

Your stylin? So the style is yours? Now your talkin'.

Opposite: Horrible what happens when your apostrophe drops.

Its newest stars. Its. *It's* means *it is.*

You got people? I have people, thanks.

Three
∧

FASHION STATEMENTS

Put this T-shirt in the trash.

Our worst nightmare: a missing apostrophe.

Teaching babies the wrong places to
put apostrophes is child abuse.

It's not cheating if your drunk cousin does it? Ohh, if *you're* drunk. Say what you mean, kids.

Oops! Some mistakes are worse than others.

I ♥ the proper use of apostrophes.

No, no, no, no! *Want* does *not* want an apostrophe!

Four
∧

PARKING, DRIVING, CARS, AND TRAVEL

Does *privite* rhyme with *invite*?

Has anyone seen two missing *E*'s?

Don't drink and make road signs.

If the bus brakes, the glass
brakes as well.

This is one of the first things visitors see upon entering the United States. You'd think that the grammar and punctuation would be impeccable, right? Provide your what?

Blind drivers, corner slowly. Drivers who can see, corner at full speed.

The gate is closed, people. *Closed*.

So the cars park themselves?

Kids without gas have to sit
in the car.

Canada *cannot* fit in a suitcase.

You could have saved yourself some space on this sign!

The road less traveled, probably to your right.

Just because you pronounce it that way
doesn't mean it's spelled that way.

"Please remain seated until tender is dock." Hmm. "Please remain seated until the dock is tendered?" Who knows?

You'd think traffic signals painted on the ground should be spelled correctly. Especially a word like *parking*.

We wonder what being trespassed would feel like.

Parking quietly, however, is allowed.

08/15/2008

I before *E*, except after *C*. Write that one hundred times over while you *think* about what you've done.

Five
∧

NEWSPAPERS

AND

BOOKS

Canada
2006. In
jumped

Cana
increas
capturi
truck n
Saskat
cent o
increas
but in
percen

The
includ
reason
for pe
vans o
The simila
150 and Ram

PHOTO COURTESY OF CHRYSLER LLC

Dodge has upgraded teh interior of the new Ram.

Proofreader on vacation?

C'mon, people. You work at a newspaper,
you should know better!

Either the magazines are kind, or
there should be an *s* at the end
of *kind*. And *magazines*.

Even the news store needs to relearn the apostrophe chapter from 2nd grade.
We're disappointed in you, Hearsall.

There should probably be some punctuation in that bottom line.

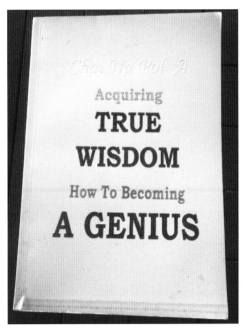

Acquiring

TRUE

WISDOM

How To Becoming

A GENIUS

First step: Hey Genius—watch your grammar.

Six
∧

EDUMACATION

Well, it's only Junior High—there's still
time to learn the difference between
your and *you're*.

Vive l'indépendance!

Is there a spelling category for the Wolverine achievement awards?

Student government needs a grammar check.

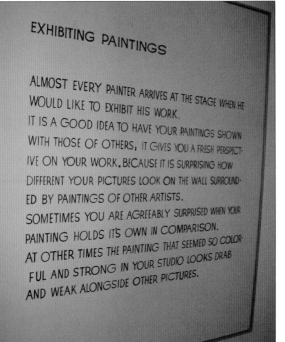

EXHIBITING PAINTINGS

ALMOST EVERY PAINTER ARRIVES AT THE STAGE WHEN HE
WOULD LIKE TO EXHIBIT HIS WORK.
IT IS A GOOD IDEA TO HAVE YOUR PAINTINGS SHOWN
WITH THOSE OF OTHERS; IT GIVES YOU A FRESH PERSPECT-
IVE ON YOUR WORK. BECAUSE IT IS SURPRISING HOW
DIFFERENT YOUR PICTURES LOOK ON THE WALL SURROUND-
ED BY PAINTINGS OF OTHER ARTISTS.
SOMETIMES YOU ARE AGREEABLY SURPRISED WHEN YOUR
PAINTING HOLDS ITS OWN IN COMPARISON.
AT OTHER TIMES THE PAINTING THAT SEEMED SO COLOR-
FUL AND STRONG IN YOUR STUDIO LOOKS DRAB
AND WEAK ALONGSIDE OTHER PICTURES.

You'd think the Museum
of Modern Art in
Washington, DC, would
double-check for
grammatical mistakes.

Teaching children bad punctuation is unacceptable.

Consistency aside, this is still wrong.

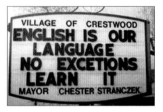

No excetions, eh? How about
learning to spell *exceptions?*

Spirt? Wonder what they're spirting.

Seven
^

LOST
IN
TRANSLATION

Good luck in Mexico! Correct English grammar,
but a shabby translation at best.

I sale, you sale, we sale . . . stams?

Don't tripe when you're drunkenly walking.

This has got to be the wittiest restroom I have ever seen.

The speech delay will appreciate the free classes, we're sure.

CAUTION

Everybody; Take care of Hind!
It is the season Fawn is
born about this time. It
may be case, if you approach
him, his mother deer being
full of maternal love gives
you a kick by her forfeet.

Don't get kicked; take care of your hind!

Someone made a stamp that says "Norrh"?

Somebody paid for this sign.

Oh, of course. Restrooms are
toward your behind.

Somebody call Dateline!

Watch out for the slippery trip hazard.

"PLEASE DO NOT DISPOSE OF SANITARY NAPKINS, OR BROWN PAPER IN COMMODE"

Where *should* the brown paper go?

Bewere, but happy dining!

It's a holy place. Leave your
cigarettes and guns outside.

Coming soon: Java Judo. You're
wellcome to that also.

Enjoy me as much as you want.

This sign brought to you from Thaisland.

WARNING
THIS CHAIR CAN ONLY LOAD 225 LBS/102KG MAXIMUM.PLEASE DO NOT APPLY ANY LOADS OVER THE ABOVE WT. OR YOU MAY CAUSE THE CHAIR BROKEN & INJURE YOURSELF.
CF-400

All together now: "to be, or not to be" broken.

因重要活动，给您的参观游览带来不便，敬请原谅。

Because the important activity, is gone on a sightseeing tour by you bring about forgiving inconveniently, please.

故宫博物院
The Palace Museum

Exhibits like sightseeing as much everyone else.

Eight
^

SAY

WHAT?

I am so scared of poltergiests. There and back.

"Claw don't move foreward nor backward."
At least the apostrophe is correct.

This dryer *doesn't* heat up.

If you're tored, you're unvalid.

A case of the mix-and-match vowel syndrome.

They're removing the beach?

Unfortunately, we think this one was on purpose.

George must be gorgeous.

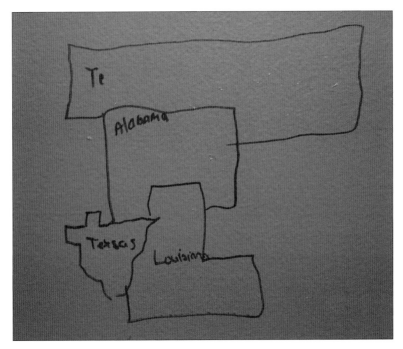

Nice drawing; unfortunate spelling.

Isn't spell check automatic when you type signs?

That sign be broke, too.

I stopped reading, thank goodness.

The adverb is dying. Use *ly*, people, before it disappears completely.

Protect hurricanes and global warming
while you're at it.

Everythings's cheap! And
hopelessly incorrect!

What do you think a "personnel
watermelon" is?

So, in other words, someone is getting very near for an event involving running. But it's ok, no need to be sorry for something so in convenience.

The quotation marks do not make
us trust this store.

We don't know what he's trying to say, but we
do know that *globle* and *analisis* aren't words.

Don't knock it 'til you've tried it.

Well, hotdawhg!

You're freacking us out here.

"Frow papers int the basket." Got that?

Glad someone is listening!

Nine

Λ

APOSTROPHE
CATASTROPHE

Free kids! And their coloring, we suppose.

FOR YOUR
SAFETY DO
NOT WALK
ON THE ROOF
TAKE EXTRA CARE
WHEN WALKING ALONG
GUNWALE'S
(SIDES OF BOAT)

Also take care when it comes to plurals and possessives.

Please return smokers and blankets to this basket when you're through with them.

These forty-eight cents belong to the bananas!

Go have a shot of whiskey. Your grammar needs help.

We think they meant *parties*.

This toilet must be for
one specific boy.

Please, just use any of the abundant extra apostrophes from this chapter.

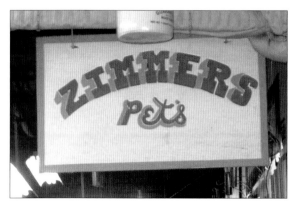

Take the apostrophe from *pet's* and move it to
Zimmer's. Much better.

I'm in a hurry to fix that
bastardized *your're*.

Mow'in Joe's
Lawn Cutting

$35.00 a cut
Includes:
mowing, weekwacking,
and blowing off
driveway and walkway

Does Joe mow or does the service mow Joe? Why is there an apostrophe in the middle of *mowin*'? And how do you wack a week?

Apostrophe eraser please? *Tellers*. That's better.

This sign is full of opportunities to correct its punctuation.

PLEASE TUCK YOU'RE LACES IN THANK YOU

You are laces? Really now. That's interesting.

This sign makes us think we haven't progressed all that much since the pirates.

Young LADIES;
   PLEASE TELL YOUR
mother's where frank's
place is, She's The only
who will pick up AFTER You.
                    Jerry

We're having visions of Dr. Seuss's Whos.

Ten
∧

MISCELLANEOUS

Welcomme to this bar! Come in and get a
free apostrophe!

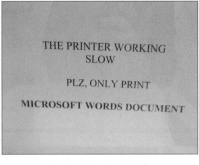

Slowly. Adverbs, people.

Natalie and Mark was here. Or were here. Whatever.

There's no spelling test for voting, thank goodness.

Pray for the birds of prey.

The buzzard is not working
It rings but the door does not
open.

Everyone, you didn't pray hard enough, the buzzard is not
working. The buzzer, however, is of questionable status.

We hope this sign was on sale (or on sael).

If you have this sign in front of your house, you might be a redneck.

You can block the door closed, but not open.

This is another lamination abomination.

Even your dog and cat are making faces at your incompetent spelling. Very unproffessional!

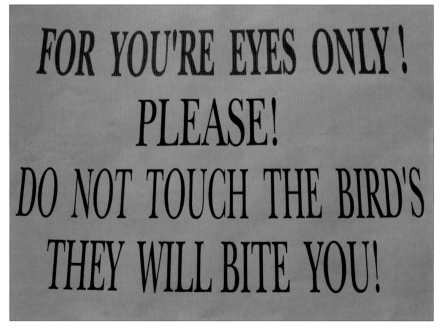

FOR YOU'RE EYES ONLY !
PLEASE!
DO NOT TOUCH THE BIRD'S
THEY WILL BITE YOU!

The birds will bite you, since you are all eyes. And don't touch the bird's what?

MASSAGE...?	TIME	PRICE
Reflex massage	45 min	150 L.E
Sportive massage	45 min	150 L.E
Shiatsu massage	45 min	150 L.E
Tahi massage	45 min	150 L.E
Swedish massage	45 min	150 L.E
Acupressure massage	45 min	150 L.E
Acupuncher massage	45 min	150 L.E

For more information and a reservation
Please contact the reception .

You puncher, you brought her.

As opposed to a
non-male man?

The beach does what?

Waving the sign won't distract us from the woefully inadequate grammar featured on it.

We'd rather not suffocate while watching TV.

Get spell check, dude!

PHOTO CREDITS

Andrew Albertson: 110 (right)
Trish Amee: 133 (left)
Michelle Arney: 9 (right)
Marianne Baker: 79 (left)
Amanda Brzezowski: 124 (left)
Kristin Burke: 21
Megan Jayne Butler: 75 (left)
Brittany Candeger: 29
Kevin Challenger: 36
Michelle Cosper: 91 (left)
Lori Crichter: 3
Christopher Curzio: 8, 121 (right)
Lisa Davis: 16 (right)
Amy Dee: 130
Elaine K. de la Mata: 136
Mary Dempsey: 25
Octavio Diaz: 103
Steve Dinn: 75 (left)
Alan Duda: 46
Danielle Dumanoir: 138 (left)

Jessica Rachel Dunlop: 19, 63, 95
Rowena Evans: 35 (top)
Tiffany Fox: 79 (right), 94 (left)
Kira Gaber: 142 (left)
Samantha Garofalo: 91 (right)
Kelly Gilbert: 112 (right), 116 (right)
Lauren Gray: 114
Amy Griffin: 100 (right)
Karrie Guthrie: 44, 137 (right),
    143 (left)
Matthew B. Harnick: 142 (right)
Paul Harrison: 69
Carly Heims: 11, 12, 89
Meredith Hilliard: 47, 140
Ben Hogenauer: 134 (right)
Becky Hughes: 57
Thomas Humphries: 31 (right)
Emily Hunt: 88
Allison Hussey: 43
Samantha Iyer: 15 (right), 102 (left)

Juliet Jackson: 110 (left)
Sara Jenkins: 7 (right)
Kathryn Johnston: 84
Annie Jones: 5 (right)
Lauren K. Keller: 135
Richard Kessler: 144
Kashif Siddiq Khawaja: 111
John King: 60
Michael Kirshner: 10 (right)
Tony Klose: 9 (left), 26 (left)
Rebecca Koger: 104
Todd Lanouette: 106 (left)
Jeanne LaSala: 92
Andy Lawson: 45, 55 (right)
Nancy Little: 32
Mara Lopez: 56
E. C. MacGregor Boyle: 139
Jodie Madsen: 62 (right)
Michel Marizco: 83
Virginia Minehart: 115

Tatiana Morales: 86
Meridith Morris: 54 (right)
Lynn Moynahan: 128 (left)
Patrick Mullen: 80
Caro Nally: 62 (left)
Amy Neely: 100 (left)
Ariel Nieland: 109
Nicola Nunweiler: 53 (left)
David James O'Connor: 55 (left)
Erin O'Connor: 30
Jayne O'Connor: 15 (left)
o.D. in Dubai: 68 (left)
Andrea Olsen: 5 (left), 137 (left)
Justin Pavlischek: 85 (left)
Corina Pena-Gregori: 116 (left)
Adam Polanski: 125 (left), 126
Jill Pruitt: 96
Diana Quick: 58 (right)
Daniela Rapp: 17, 18, 20, 39,
    90 (right), 94 (right), 113
Brittany Reelitz: 34
Stephanie Reichman: 35 (bottom)
Ben Rene: 10 (left)
Chuck Rhine: 14

J. Michael Riley: 59 (left)
Ric Robinson: 7 (left), 27, 120
Shannon Rothwell: 61
Jackie Rudolph: 16 (left)
Matthew Russell: 6
Karen Savage: 102 (right)
Joseph Schlesinger: 54 (left),
    58 (left), 68 (right), 70, 90
    (left)
Suzie Seaman: 49
Meryl Seidel: 26 (right)
Brian Shepherd: 112 (left)
Wakeela Simpson: 64
David Slenk: 77
Brian Smith: 128 (right)
Gregg Sperling: 76 (right)
Jennifer Spry: 93 (right), 141,
    143 (right)
Juliet Stanton: 85 (right)
Ty Storey: 31 (left), 106 (right)
Rob Stradling: 123
Anita Summers: 87
Anne Swearingen: 13 (right)
Dan Taubert: 13 (left)

Sarah Taylor: 124 (right)
Stephanie Thomas: 33
Jenni Thompson: 107
Kearnan Tomlinson: 59 (right)
Erin Townsend: 28
Stephanie Turner: 125 (right)
Luke Valentine: 93 (left), 121
    (left), 134 (left)
Kathryn VanDyk: 108
Helen Van Wagoner: 48
Frank Viscotti: 99
Tara Walker: 78
Kelly Warren: 138 (right)
Jayne Werry: 67, 127
Colton Wheeler: 4, 133 (right)
Heather Wilk: 75 (right)
Leah Wilkinson: 119
Jessica Wilson: 53 (right)
Margie Winn: 129
Wendy Jade Wong: 71, 122
Sarah Wood: 105
Caroline Worsley: 38
Terry Wreghitt: 101
Zoe Yarborough: 37